# Bread

## in a

# Flowerpot

A Recipe Collection
Jackie Gannaway

Published in Austin, TX by COOKBOOK CUPBOARD,
P.O. Box 50053, Austin, TX 78763 (512) 477-7070

ISBN 1-885597-17-7

NOTICE: The information contained in this book is true, complete, and accurate to the best of my knowledge. All recommendations and suggestions are made without any guaranty on the part of the editor or Cookbook Cupboard. The editor and publisher disclaim any liability incurred in connection with the use of this information.

Artwork by Mosey 'N Me    1436 Baird    Katy, Texas 77493    (713) 391-2281

# Kitchen Crafts Collection

## Mail Order Information

To order a copy of this book send a check for $3.95 + $1.50 for shipping per order (TX residents add 8 % sales tax) to Cookbook Cupboard, P.O. Box 50053, Austin, TX 78763. Send a note asking for this title by name. If you would like a descriptive list of all the fun titles in The Kitchen Crafts Collection, send a note asking for an order blank.

A title readers of this book might enjoy is "Cake in a Jar". It is a collection of 20 recipes for baking cakes and breads in one pint canning jars. The cakes are actually sealed and have a shelf life of several months.

There is information on pg. 32 of this book on ordering glazed flowerpots from Cookbook Cupboard.

All the Kitchen Crafts titles are $3.95. Shipping is $1.50 per order up to $30.00.

# Why Am I Baking in a Flowerpot?

Baking and serving breads in flowerpots is fun and different. These breads are perfect for summertime luncheons, meetings, wedding showers, house warming gifts, bake sales and bazaars, family reunions, picnics, barbecues, and much more. Treat your weekend guests to a fancy "bed and breakfast" breakfast on your patio with some flowerpot breads.

## What Will This Book Tell Me?

This book has complete instructions for baking and serving in clay flowerpots and thorough directions for preparing the flowerpots for baking. It has recipes for several quick breads, bread mixes and even ways to bake refrigerated roll and biscuit dough in flowerpots.

The simplest way to bake in flowerpots is to have a flowerpot that is glazed on the inside with a food safe glaze. These flowerpots are available in catalogs and occasionally in crafts stores or gourmet shops. They will probably become more widely available in the next few years.

You can glaze your own flowerpots and I strongly recommend it. Specific glazing directions are on pgs. 8-9.

If you don't use glazed flowerpots, you will need to line the unglazed ones with heavy duty foil. Directions for that are on pg. 6.

Flowerpots are oven, microwave and dishwasher safe.

Make up some of the bread mixes from this book and package them in a flowerpot. They are perfect for gifts and for selling at bake sales. They are also perfect for keeping on hand as last minutes gifts because they have a long shelf life.

For a list of all recipes in this book, see the index on pg. 32.

---

Please read all the introductory pages before you prepare any of the recipes. It is not complicated but there are several things to know before you begin.

3

# What Size Flowerpot?

The recipes and mixes in this book are designed for "standard 4" flowerpots". They are 4" tall with a 4 1/4" diameter opening. The muffin size breads are designed for "standard 3" flowerpots". They are 3 1/4" tall with a 3" diameter opening. ("Standard" is a flowerpot term for the shape. Standard pots are a little taller than the squattier "azalea" pots.) You can bake in the azalea pots, but you will have to figure out the amount of batter to use and the baking time. I limited the scope of this book to the standard 4" pots for a bread that would serve 2 to 4 people and the 3" pot as an individual "muffin" size serving.

Buy flowerpots at discount stores, home centers or garden centers. They can help you find these sizes.

 ## Can I Bake in Any Flowerpot?

You don't know where the flowerpots you buy were made. You don't know the materials used in making the flowerpots. They are probably not made of a "food safe" material. You must either:

1. Buy a flower pot designed for baking. Buy these at gourmet shops. Be sure the size is what is called for in the recipes in this book.

2. Glaze your own flowerpots by following the instructions on pgs. 8-9. Glazing the inside of the flowerpot with a food safe glaze keeps the food from touching the unglazed clay, allows for better baking and browning, and allows the bread to slide out.

3. Use any flowerpot (new, please!), but line it with HEAVY DUTY ALUMINUM FOIL. Follow the instructions on pg. 6 for lining with foil.

---

NEVER, EVER BAKE IN A FLOWERPOT UNLESS IT MEETS ONE OF THE CRITERIA ABOVE.
It may not be made of food safe material.

---

# How Can I Decorate My Flowerpot Breads?

The possibilities are endless for using these breads to add distinction and fun to your meal or event.

Let them be part of the centerpiece. Place them among pots of blooming flowers (vary the heights by standing things on top of upside down flowerpots).

They can be favors to be taken home with the guests after being displayed in the centerpiece.

Lay small trowels, seed packets and other garden items among the flowerpots.

Wrap the pot with a colorful napkin, cloth square or a large paper doily. Secure it with a rubber band and then tie with raffia or ribbon. Stick in small real flowers or silk flowers between the pot and the fabric or doily.

# How Do I Serve a Flowerpot Bread?

Leave these breads in the flowerpots to serve. For individual "muffin" size, the person eating can slide the bread out of the flowerpot onto their plate. They might need to use a plain table knife to loosen the bread from the side of a glazed pot. The foil lined pots allow the bread to slide out and then the foil is removed and discarded.

You can use your regular dessert plates for serving or you can use some flowerpot saucers (glazed or lined with waxed paper).

To serve the 4" flowerpots: Place them on the table on a plate or flowerpot saucer as described above. As your guests watch, you slide the bread out and slice it at the table (with a serrated knife). Slice bread crosswise into round slices. You may need to loosen the bread before taking it to the table by running a plain table knife between the bread and the pot (for glazed pots - for foil lined pots, lift out by the foil.)

You can serve butters or cream cheeses (pg. 31) in a 1 1/2" flowerpot (glazed or foil lined) for each individual person, or in a 2 1/2" flowerpot for the whole table.

# How To Season Flowerpots

Before using flowerpots for baking you should "season" them. This procedure helps keep grease streaks and fingerprints from showing.

Rub all inside and outside surfaces of flowerpots with shortening (on paper towels). (Don't season the inside of the glazed flowerpots - it is not necessary.) Wipe off excess shortening.

Heat empty flowerpots in 350° oven for 15 minutes. You still have to line seasoned unglazed flowerpots with foil.

## How to Line Flowerpots with Heavy Duty Foil

Use heavy duty foil only. That is a particular type of foil and it will say so on the package. Turn the flowerpot upside down on your countertop. Pull off a large piece of heavy duty foil and press it over the flowerpot, pushing to conform the foil to the shape of the pot. Remove the foil.

Turn the flowerpot right side up and place the shaped foil inside the flowerpot. Use scissors to trim the excess foil from the edges of the flowerpot.

Before baking generously spray the foil with cooking spray.

## How Many Flowerpots Does One Recipe Make?

Most of the recipes in this book make four 4" flowerpots or eight to ten 3" muffin size flowerpots. In most recipes, instructions for how much batter and time to bake is given for both sizes.

You can make some of each size - for example, two 4" pots and four 3" muffin size pots. Cook them all at the same, but set the timer for the shorter time for the muffin size first.

# How to Bake Bread in a Flowerpot

## Preparing the Flowerpot - Unglazed

Before you bake in an unglazed flowerpot, you must line it with heavy duty foil (see pg. 6 for exact directions).

Spray the foil generously with cooking spray so it will peel easily away from the baked bread. To serve these breads, turn the flowerpot upside down to allow the bread to slide out. Peel away the foil. Individuals can do this to the muffin size breads. The person who is going to cut the bread peels away the foil from the larger breads.

Place all filled flowerpots on a baking sheet in the oven. This will catch any batter that drips out of the hole in the flowerpot as well as help the flowerpots balance on the oven rack.

## Preparing the Flowerpot - Glazed

Before you bake in a glazed flowerpot, you must cover the hole. Cut a square piece of foil a little wider than the bottom of the flowerpot. Turn the pot upside down and press the foil against the bottom and up the sides a little. Remove this from the outside of the flowerpot and place it inside. Press it as securely to the sides of the pot as you can. This forms a little "cup" to keep any of the thinner batters from oozing out the hole. Spray the inside of the flowerpot generously with cooking spray.

You may need to use a plain table knife to loosen the baked bread from the glazed pot. Do this before you bring it to the table, so it will come out easily when you are serving it.

# Glazing Your Own Flowerpots
## Getting Started

Glazing flowerpots is very simple. However, there are several steps involved. Start by stopping by a ceramics shop (find them in the Yellow Pages). Tell them what you have in mind and show them a plain flowerpot of the size you want to glaze. Ask if they will fire it for you in their kiln. Most shop operators know that clay pots are safe to go in kilns. The shop will be happy to know that the bottom of the flowerpot will not be glazed so they can sit it right on kiln shelf.

Buy a small container of food safe glaze and a brush at the ceramics shop. You can use white glaze or a color (as long as it is food safe), but I prefer clear glaze. Clear is more forgiving of first time mistakes and simply enhances the terra cotta color of the flowerpot. If you are planning your flowerpots for a particular party or occasion and have a color scheme then go ahead and glaze the pots to match the color scheme. (Just be sure the glaze says "food safe" on the container.)

If you are going to follow the recipes in this book you will need 4" "standard" flowerpots for the breads and 3" "standard" flowerpots for the muffins. A good number for your personal use is four 4" pots and eight 3" muffin size pots. You should also glaze several flowerpot saucers of varying sizes to use as serving dishes and 4 each of the tiny 1 1/2" flowerpots and the 2 1/2" flowerpots (for butter and/or cream cheese).

Buy flowerpots at discount stores, home centers, or garden centers.

## Painting Flowerpots

If you want to paint a design on the outside of a flowerpot and still be able to bake breads in it use Delta® Air Dry Permanent Enamel. First wipe the area with Delta's new surface cleaner and paint following the directions on the paint. This paint can take temperatures to 350° and is available at crafts stores.

# Glazing Your Own Flowerpots
## Applying the Glaze

The glaze is a liquid that is thinner than paint. When it is dry, but not fired, it looks like you have painted the inside of the flowerpot with flat wall paint.

Get a container ready for the glaze and a container (like a medium size shallow plastic food container) to work over to catch drips.

Cover an area on a table with newspapers or paper towels for the pots to sit while they dry. Place a wire rack (like a rack for cooling cookies or a modular shelving rack that is has rubber coated wires or even your oven rack) on top of the newspapers.

For every cup of glaze thin with 3 tsp. of water. This makes a "pouring" consistency. Reserve some of the glaze in its original consistency for the rim of the pot.

Put a piece of masking tape on the outside over the drain hole.

Hold the flowerpot in one hand and pour the glaze into it. Rotate the pot to coat the entire inside with glaze. Pour and shake the excess glaze back into the container you are using. Set the flowerpot upside down on the rack for the excess glaze to drain out. When the glaze is dry turn the pot right side up and smooth the glaze on the rim with a damp sponge.

Your glaze will be white at this point. It needs to be opaque. You don't want to see the pot through the glaze - that means you have not coated it sufficiently. You can put on another coat of glaze if you think your first coat is too thin.

After glaze is dry, use a wet rag to wipe off streaks or fingerprints of glaze that are on the outside of the flowerpot.

Take your flowerpots to the ceramics shop to be fired. They will fire at temperature "Cone 06".The kiln is usually fired overnight, so you will get your pots back in a day or two. When you get them back they will be slick inside and won't have to be lined with foil for baking.

9

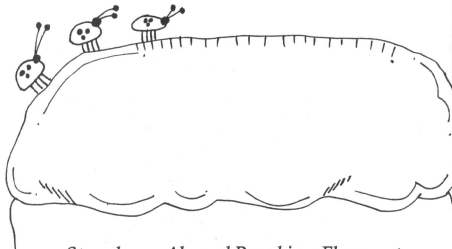

## Strawberry Almond Bread in a Flowerpot

| | |
|---|---|
| 1 1/2 cups flour | 2 eggs |
| 3/4 tsp. baking soda | 1/2 cup oil |
| 1/2 tsp. salt | 1 (10 oz.) pkg. frozen |
| 2 tsp. cinnamon | strawberries, thawed, |
| 1 cup sugar | not drained |
| 3/4 cup chopped almonds | 1 tsp. almond extract |

1. Place first 6 ingredients in large mixing bowl and blend with a whisk.
2. In another mixing bowl, beat eggs with a fork. Add oil and mix until blended.
3. Add thawed strawberries and their juice and extract to egg mixture. Mix well.
4. Add wet mixture to dry mixture, stirring just until blended.
5. Place 1 1/3 cups batter into each of four 4" prepared (pg. 7) flowerpots.
6. Bake in preheated 325° oven for 55 to 65 minutes. For muffin size breads place 1/2 cup batter into prepared 3" flowerpots and bake 40 to 45 minutes at 325°.

Makes three 4" flowerpots or seven 3" muffin size flowerpots.

## Peach Bread in a Flowerpot

1 (16oz.) bag frozen peaches, thawed and undrained
1/2 cup sugar
2 cups flour
1 tsp. baking powder
1 tsp. baking soda
1/4 tsp. salt

1 tsp. cinnamon
1 1/2 cups sugar
1/3 cup shortening
2 eggs
1 tsp. vanilla
1 cup chopped pecans (opt.)

1. Place thawed peaches and their juice and 1/2 cup sugar in food processor and puree.
2. Place dry ingredients in a mixing bowl and blend with a whisk.
3. Place 1 1/2 cups sugar and shortening in another mixing bowl. Mix with electric mixer until well blended.
4. Add eggs and vanilla. Mix well with electric mixer.
5. Add peaches to egg mixture and mix.
6. Add dry ingredients and optional pecans and mix until just moistened.
7. Place 1 1/4 cups batter into each of four 4" prepared (pg. 7) flowerpots.
8. Bake in preheated 325° oven for 45 to 55 minutes.
   For muffin size breads, place 1/2 cup batter in prepared 3" flowerpots and bake 40 minutes at 325°.

Makes four 4" flowerpots or ten 3" muffin size flowerpots.

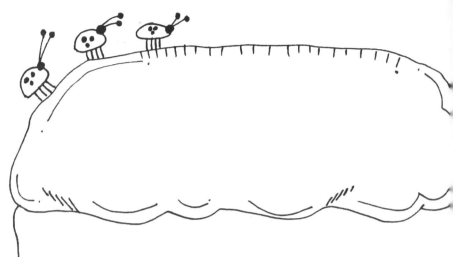

## Spiced Apple Date Bread in a Flowerpot

1 1/2 cups buttermilk
1 1/2 tsp. baking soda
3 cups flour
4 tsp. baking powder
3/4 tsp. salt
1 Tb. cinnamon
2 eggs

3/4 cup sugar
6 Tb. margarine, melted
1 (8 oz.) box chopped dates,
   (2 cups)
2 cups chopped, peeled apples
Topping: 3 Tb. sugar
3/4 tsp. cinnamon

1. Mix buttermilk and soda in medium bowl. Set aside.
2. Place dry ingredients in large bowl and blend with a whisk.
3. Place eggs in medium bowl. Beat lightly.
4. Add sugar and melted margarine to eggs. Mix well.
5. Add egg mixture to buttermilk mixture.
6. Add wet ingredients to dry ingredients. Mix until just
    blended.
7. Add dates and apples. Mix.
8. Place 1 1/4 cup batter each in four 4" prepared(pg. 7)
    flowerpots.
9. Bake in preheated 350° oven for 40 to 45 minutes.
    For muffin size breads, place 1/2 cup + 1 Tb. batter
    into prepared 3" flowerpots and bake 30 to 35 minutes
    at 350°.

Makes four 4" flowerpots or ten 3" muffin size flowerpots.

## Apple Butter Bread in a Flowerpot

1 stick + 2 Tb. margarine
1 cup packed brown sugar
1 egg and 1 egg white
scant 1 cup buttermilk
2 tsp. soda
2 1/4 cups flour

1 tsp. cinnamon
1 tsp. nutmeg
1 tsp. allspice
1/4 tsp. cloves
1 cup + 2 Tb. apple butter
1/2 cup chopped pecans, (opt.)

1. Place margarine and brown sugar in large bowl. Mix with electric mixer until well blended.
2. Add eggs and mix well.
3. Place buttermilk and soda in small bowl. Mix. Set aside.
4. Place flour and spices in medium bowl. Blend with a whisk.
5. Add dry ingredients to egg mixture alternately with the buttermilk mixture, beginning and ending with flour.
6. Add apple butter and pecans and mix gently.
7. Place 1 1/4 cups batter into each of four 4" prepared (pg. 7) flowerpots.
8. Bake in preheated 350° oven for 35 to 45 minutes. For muffin size breads place 1/2 cup + 1 Tb. batter into prepared 3" muffin size flowerpots and bake 25 to 30 minutes at 350°.

Makes four 4" flowerpots or nine 3" muffin sized flowerpots.

13

## *Bread Mixes*

This book has three bread mixes - an Onion Dill Bread Mix, a Cinnamon Raisin Bread Mix and a Parmesan Herb Beer Bread Mix. The Onion Dill and the Cinnamon Raisin both need an egg and some milk added and the Parmesan Herb Mix needs some beer added.

Make as many mixes as you wish. Each mix makes one 4" flowerpot of bread.

These breads are excellent gifts because they are very easy for you to make and easy for the recipient to bake.

Since the mixes are measured for baking in flowerpots you should package them in a flowerpot as part of your gift. You can glaze the pots (pgs. 8-9) or give plain flowerpots with a copy of the instructions for preparing flowerpots for baking from pg. 7.

To give a mix (or two) in a flowerpot, place the mix bag with the spice packet attached into a flowerpot. Place a flowerpot saucer upside down on top of the flowerpot. Tie it all together with some raffia, a silk flower, and a little card saying "Onion Dill Bread Mix" and "To" and "From". You can add a bright cloth napkin inside the flowerpot for more festive color (and a seed packet to carry out the garden theme).

You need to copy the instructions "To Mix the Bread" from the recipe and include it with the mix. If you want the recipient to have a copy of the mix ingredients as well the copyright on this book has been "relaxed" to allow a few copies for personal use (see copyright page). You can have a full service copy shop copy the page right onto colored cardstock.

If you want to make one of the mix recipes, but not as a mix you mix the dry ingredients in a small bowl and add the egg and milk or the beer called for. Mix following the instructions under "To Mix the Bread". Mix one batch at a time - one batch fills one 4" flowerpot.

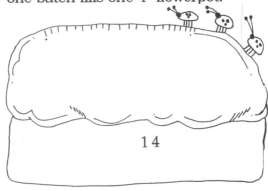

14

# Cinnamon Raisin Bread Mix

1 1/3 cups Bisquick®          1 tsp. cinnamon
1/4 cup packed brown sugar    1/3 cup golden raisins

1. Place first 3 ingredients in a mixing bowl and blend with a whisk.
2. Stir in raisins.
3. Place mix in heavy plastic zipper bag.
4. Tie on a recipe card that tells how to make the bread (instructions below). Include a copy of pg. 7 on flowerpot preparations.

### Cinnamon Raisin Bread Mix
### To Mix the Bread

1. Empty mix into a mixing bowl.
2. Add 1 egg and 1/3 cup milk.
3. Mix until just blended.
4. Pour batter into one prepared 4" flowerpot.
5. Bake at 375° for 40 to 45 minutes.

Makes one 4" flowerpot - Cinnamon Raisin Bread.

## *Parmesan Herb Beer Bread Mix*

1 1/3 cups Bisquick®
2 Tb. sugar

1 1/4 tsp. Italian herb
seasoning
2 Tb. grated Parmesan

1. Place Bisquick and sugar in small mixing bowl and blend with a whisk.
2. Place Bisquick mixture in a small plastic zipper bag.
3. Place herb seasoning and Parmesan on a small square of plastic wrap. Bring up sides of plastic wrap and secure into a little packet with a rubber band. Tie a ribbon around rubber band.
4. Tie on a recipe card that tells how to make the bread (instructions below). Include a copy of pg. 7 on flowerpot preparation.

---

### Parmesan Herb Beer Bread Mix
### To Mix the Bread

1. Empty mix and spice packet into a mixing bowl.
2. Blend with a whisk.
3. Add 3/4 cup beer and mix rapidly for 30 seconds.
4. Pour batter into one prepared 4" flowerpot
5. Bake at 375° for 40 to 45 minutes.
Makes one 4" flowerpot - Parmesan Herb Beer Bread.

## Onion Dill Bread Mix

1 1/3 cups Bisquick®
1 Tb. Golden Onion
   Recipe Secrets® packet

1/4 tsp. coarse black pepper
1/2 tsp. dried dillweed

1. Place Bisquick in a small plastic zipper bag.
2. Place remaining 3 ingredients on a small square of plastic wrap. Bring up sides of plastic wrap and secure into a little packet with a rubber band. Tie a ribbon around rubber band.
3. Attach this spice packet to zipper bag with a stapler or by cutting a hole and tying on with ribbon.
4. Tie on a recipe card that tells how to make the bread (instructions below). Include a copy of pg. 7 on flowerpot preparation.

---

### Onion Dill Bread Mix
#### To Mix the Bread

1. Empty mix and spice packet into a mixing bowl.
2. Blend with a whisk.
3. Add 1 egg and 1/3 cup milk.
4. Mix until just blended.
5. Pour batter into one prepared 4" flowerpot.
6. Bake at 375° for 35 to 40 minutes.
Makes one 4" flowerpot of Onion Dill Bread.

---

## Bell Pepper and Onion Monkey Bread
## in a Flowerpot

4 refrigerated canned biscuits
2 Tb. margarine, melted
2 Tb. Lipton Golden Onion
   Recipe Secrets®

1/3 cup chopped red
   or green bell pepper
3 green onions, chopped
   with tops

1. Cut biscuits into quarters. Place in mixing bowl.
2. Mix margarine with onion mix and pour over biscuits.
3 Add chopped pepper and onion. Toss well to
   distribute pepper and onion evenly.
4. Place all in one 4" prepared (pg. 7) flowerpot.
5. Bake in preheated 375° oven for 30 minutes. Cover
   loosely with foil for the last 10 minutes so bread won't
   overbrown. Serve immediately.

Makes one 4" flowerpot.

## Cinnamon Nut Monkey Bread

4 refrigerated canned biscuits
1 Tb. sugar mixed with
1/2 tsp. cinnamon
1 Tb. chopped pecans (opt.)

2 Tb. brown sugar
2 Tb. margarine
1 tsp. water

1. Cut biscuits into quarters. Place in mixing bowl.
2. Sprinkle with cinnamon sugar mixture and pecans.
   Toss to coat well.
3. Place all in one 4" prepared (pg. 7) flowerpot.
4. Mix brown sugar, margarine and water well in
   a small microsafe dish. Microwave 1 minute.
5. Pour margarine mixture over biscuits in flowerpot.
6. Bake in preheated 350° oven for 25 minutes.
   Serve immediately.

Makes one 4" flowerpot.

19

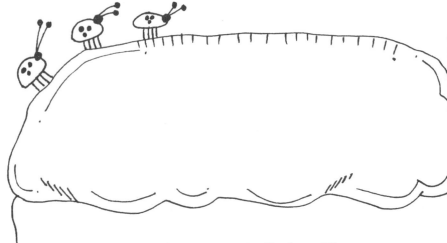

## Simple Cinnamon Rolls in a Flowerpot

1 (8 count) can crescent rolls
2 Tb. butter, melted
1/3 cup sugar

1/4 tsp. cinnamon
Glaze: 1/3 cup powdered
  sugar mixed with
  1 tsp. water

1. Unroll crescent roll dough on lightly floured waxed paper. Press perforations to seal.
2. Brush with melted butter.
3. Combine sugar and cinnamon and sprinkle over dough.
4. Roll up tightly, starting at long side.
5. Cut into 2" sections. Place each section into a prepared (pg. 7) 3" muffin size flowerpot.
6. Bake in preheated 350° oven for 18 to 22 minutes, watching closely.
7. Mix glaze ingredients and drizzle over cooked rolls.

Makes four 3" muffin size flowerpots.

Serve immediately in the flowerpot (placed on a plate). The person eating may need to run a plain knife around the edge of the roll to loosen. They slip the roll out of the flowerpot and place it on the plate to eat. (Can use large food safe glazed flowerpot saucers as the plates.)

# Caramel Cinnamon Rolls in a Flowerpot

1 (5 count) can Grands®      chopped pecans (opt.)
   refrigerated Caramel Rolls

1. Place one roll each in 5 prepared (pg. 7) 3" muffin size flowerpots. (Place roll on its side.)
2. Top each with the caramel frosting that comes with the rolls.
3. Sprinkle with chopped pecans if desired.
4. Bake in preheated 325° oven for 25 to 28 minutes.

    Serve immediately in the flowerpot (placed on a plate). The person eating may need to run a plain knife around the edge of the roll to loosen. They slip the roll out of the flowerpot and place it on the plate to eat. (Can use large food safe glazed flowerpot saucers as the plates.

Makes five 3" muffin size flowerpots.

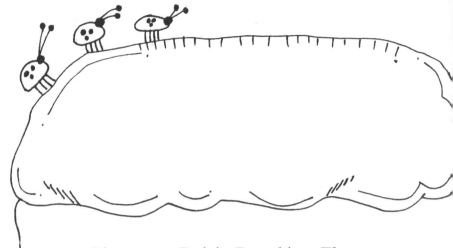

# Cinnamon Raisin Bread in a Flowerpot

| | |
|---|---|
| 1 1/2 cups golden raisins | 2 tsp. cinnamon |
| 1 1/2 cups water | 1/4 tsp. salt |
| 1 1/2 tsp. baking soda | 1 egg and 1 egg white |
| 2 1/4 cups flour | 1/2 tsp. vanilla |
| 1 1/2 cups sugar | 3/4 cup chopped pecans (opt.) |

1. Place raisins, water and baking soda in microsafe bowl. Microwave 2 minutes. Allow to cool 30 minutes.
2. Place dry ingredients in large mixing bowl. Blend with a whisk.
3. Add cooled raisin and water mixture, eggs and vanilla. Mix until just blended.
4. Add optional pecans.
5. Place 1 cup batter into each of four 4" prepared (pg. 7) flowerpots.
6. Bake in preheated 350° oven for 45 to 55 minutes. For muffin size breads place 1/3 cup batter into prepared 3" flowerpots and bake 35 to 40 minutes at 350°

Makes four 4" flowerpots or twelve 3" muffin size flowerpots.

## Cheese Bread in a Flowerpot

2 1/2 cups Bisquick®  
2 tsp. poppy seed (opt.)

1 egg, beaten  
1 cup milk  
1 cup grated cheddar

1. Place Bisquick in medium mixing bowl.
   Add optional poppy seeds and blend well.
2. Add egg and milk. Mix until jest blended.
3. Add grated cheddar and mix vigorously for
   1 minute.
4. Place 1 1/3 cup batter into each of two 4" prepared
   (pg. 7) flowerpots.
5. Bake in preheated 350° oven for 45 to 55 minutes.
   For muffin size breads place 1/2 cup batter in
   prepared 3" flowerpots and bake 35 minutes at 350°.

Makes two 4" flowerpots or five 3" muffin size flowerpots.

# Dirt Cake in a Flowerpot

1 (1 lb. 4 oz.) pkg. chocolate
    sandwich cookies
1 (8 oz.) block cream cheese
1/2 stick margarine
1 cup powdered sugar
3 cups milk

1 (6 serving) chocolate
    instant pudding
1 (12 oz.) carton frozen
    whipped topping, thawed
gummi worms, flowers (silk
    or real), straws

1. Crush cookies in food processor until the crumbs resemble dirt. Set aside.
2. Mix cream cheese, margarine and powdered sugar in large bowl until well blended.
3. Mix milk and pudding in large bowl, stirring until thickened.
4. Add whipped topping and blend. Add cream cheese mixture and mix well.
5. Line a large clean clay or plastic flower pot with heavy duty foil.
6. Layer crumbs and pudding until flowerpot is filled. End with crumbs. Chill.
7. Place silk flowers in straws and push into cake. Decorate with gummi worms. Serve with a scoop. Serves 8.

# Cake and Ice Cream in a Flowerpot

| | |
|---|---|
| any flavor cake mix | chocolate sandwich cookies, |
| eggs, oil and water to | crushed |
| mix cake | gummi worms or silk or |
| any flavor ice cream | real flowers for decoration |

1. Mix cake mix following package directions.
2. Put 1/3 cup batter each in 3" prepared (pg. 7) muffin size flowerpots.
3. Bake in preheated 350° oven for 30 minutes.
4. Allow to cool. Top with ice cream.
5. Cover ice cream with crushed cookies to resemble dirt.
6. Keep in freezer until serving time. Decorate with gummi worms or flowers.

## Baking Cake Mixes in Flowerpots

Mix a favorite cake mix according to pkg. directions. Place 1 cup batter in one 4" prepared (pg. 7) flowerpot. Bake in preheated 350° oven for 40 minutes.

This will come to 1" from the top of the flowerpot. You can poke holes in the cake with a toothpick and pour a glaze over it or sprinkle powdered sugar across the top of the cake for decoration.

To make in the 3" muffin size flowerpots, use 1/2 cup batter and bake 30 minutes at 350°.

A cake mix will make five 4" flowerpots or ten 3" muffin size flowerpots.

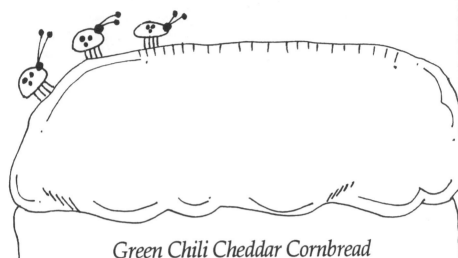

# Green Chili Cheddar Cornbread
## in a Flowerpot

| | |
|---|---|
| 1 3/4 cup buttermilk | 3/4 cup oil |
| 1 tsp. baking soda | 2 Tb. sugar |
| 1 1/2 cups cornmeal | 3/4 tsp. salt |
| 3/4 cup flour | 1 (8 oz) can cream style corn |
| 3 tsp. baking powder | 3/4 cup grated cheddar |
| 2 eggs | 1 (4 oz.) can chopped green chilies |

1. Place buttermilk and soda in small bowl and blend well. Set aside.
2. Place dry ingredients in large bowl and blend with a whisk.
3. In another bowl, beat eggs. Add oil and sugar. Mix well.
4. Add wet ingredients to dry ingredients. Blend until just moistened.
5. Add corn, grated cheddar and green chilies. Blend.
6. Place 1 cup batter each in six 4" prepared (pg. 7) flowerpots.
7. Bake in 450° oven for 35 to 45 minutes.
   To make muffin size flowerpots, place 1/2 cup batter in 3" prepared flowerpots.

Makes six 4" flowerpots or twelve 3" muffin size flowerpots.

## Deep Dish Apple Pie in a Flowerpot

| | |
|---|---|
| 1 (20 oz.) can apple pie filling | Topping: 1/2 stick margarine |
| 1 tsp. lemon juice | 2 Tb. packed brown sugar |
| 1 tsp. cinnamon | 2 Tb. sugar |
| refrigerated pie crust | 1/2 tsp. cinnamon |
| | 1/3 cup oats |

1. Place pie filling in medium bowl. Add lemon juice and cinnamon and mix well.
2. Divide apples among three 3" muffin size <u>foil lined</u> flowerpots (juice will seep out unless you line the entire flowerpot with foil). Press the apples down firmly so they will all fit (they will shrink while cooking). Cover the lip of the flowerpot with foil also.
3. Mix topping ingredients and place over the apples.
4. Cut circles of refrigerated pie crust large enough to cover the top of the flowerpot and down the lip. Cut slits for steam to escape. Place crusts on top of flowerpots.
5. Bake in preheated 350° oven for 40 to 45 minutes.

Makes three 3" muffin size flowerpots.

27

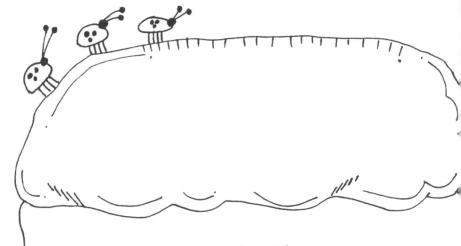

## Dinner Rolls in a Flowerpot

These dinner rolls come in a can like biscuits. They can be baked in a 4" flowerpot or in muffin sized flowerpots. They can be seasoned with herb seasoning and/or parmesan for variety.

4 refrigerated canned dinner rolls
butter flavored cooking spray

salt free herb seasoning (opt.)
parmesan (opt.)

1. Place 4 rolls in one 4" prepared (pg. 7) flowerpot. (Stand rolls on end.) Spray each one with butter flavored cooking spray.
2. Sprinkle herb seasoning and/or parmesan on top if desired.
3. Bake in preheated 350° oven for 22 to 25 minutes.

Makes one 4" flowerpot.

To make muffin size flowerpots, put 2 rolls in prepared 3" flowerpot. Bake 15 to 18 minutes at 350°.

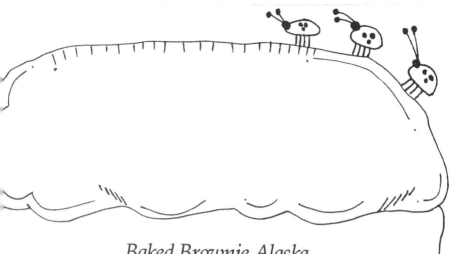

# Baked Brownie Alaska
# in a Flowerpot Saucer

| | |
|---|---|
| 1 brownie mix | vanilla ice cream |
| water | 4 egg whites |
| eggs | 12 fresh strawberries |

1. Mix brownie mix with water and eggs as called for on the package for chewy brownies.
2. Line clay saucers (4 1/2" diameter) with heavy duty foil. Grease foil. (Or used food safe glazed saucers.)
3. Spread 1/3 cup brownie batter in each saucer.
4. Bake at 350 for 25 minutes.
5. Make serving size balls of ice cream. Place ice cream balls in a flat dish and freeze hard.
6. Cool brownies completely.
7. In a small bowl, beat egg whites and sugar with electric mixer until stiff peaks form.
8. Hull and slice 2 strawberries per serving.
9. Place frozen ice cream ball on each brownie. Cover with strawberry slices.
10. Cover entire surface with meringue, being careful to seal all openings. Mound meringue high.
11. Heat at 450° for 3 to 5 minutes, watching closely.
12. Serve immediately.

A regular size brownie mix will make 5 to 6 of these. It you use a family size brownie mix use 6 egg whites for meringue.

# Apricot Nut Bread in a Paper Bag?

I thought we were talking about breads in flowerpots, what is this about a paper bag?

| | |
|---|---|
| 1 cup dried apricots | 2 cups flour |
| 1 1/4 cups sugar | 2 tsp. baking powder |
| 2 Tb. shortening | 1 tsp. baking soda |
| 1 egg | 1 tsp. salt |
| 1/2 cup orange juice | 1 cup chopped pecans |

1. Chop apricots. Place in small dish and cover with water. Soak for 30 minutes.
2. Place sugar, shortening and egg in large bowl. Beat with electric mixer. Add orange juice.
3. Place dry ingredients in medium bowl . Blend with a whisk.
4. Add dry ingredients to wet ingredients. Blend well.
5. Drain apricots and add with pecans.
6. This makes about 2 1/2 cups batter. Put 1 cup batter each into 2 prepared paper bags (see below).  Divide remaining batter evenly between the two bags so they will both have the same amount of batter.
7. Place bags on baking sheet and bake in preheated 300° oven for 65 minutes.

Use brown paper lunch bags (5" x 3" x 10") for these. Make a double "cuff" by opening the bag and folding it in half and then in half again. Crease the corners carefully with your fingers so bag keeps it rectangular shape. The bag with its cuff will be about 3 1/2" tall. Spray the bag entirely inside and out with cooking spray.

To give these cute little "bag breads" tie around the bag with raffia, making a raffia bow. Very unusual presentation.

# *Butters and Spreads*

Try giving or serving these butters with your flowerpot breads. Serve them in 1 1/2" or 2 1/2" very small flowerpots. Line them with heavy duty foil or glaze some of this small size when you are glazing the pots for the breads.

## Berry Butter

3/4 cup fresh berries*          1/2 cup powdered sugar
1 tsp. lemon juice              2 sticks butter, room temp

*cranberries, blueberries, strawberries, raspberries, blackberries.

1. Pick over berries, discarding bad berries and stems.
2. Place all ingredients in food processor and process until smooth. (For cranberry butter, process cranberries first before adding remaining ingredients.)

## Cinnamon Cream Cheese Spread

1 (8 oz.) tub soft cream cheese    1 tsp. cinnamon
1/2 stick butter, softened         1/2 tsp. vanilla
1/3 cup packed brown sugar         1/2 cup chopped pecans
                                   crystallized ginger (opt)

1. Place all ingredients except pecans in large bowl.
2. Mix with electric mixer until smooth. Stir in pecans.
   Can add chopped crystallized ginger (spice aisle).

## Spicy Spread Mix

2 Tb. salt-free herb seasoning
1 Tb. coarse black pepper

Place seasonings on a small square of plastic wrap and secure into a little packet with a rubber band. Tie a ribbon around rubber band.

Give this with instructions to mix into a 12 oz. tub of soft cream cheese and chill.

Salt-free herb seasonings are found with the spices in the store. The idea for this recipe is to have many, many spices and herbs from just one bottle. Lawrys makes one with 17 herbs and spices.

# Index